OUR HEARTSONG

OUR HEARTSONG

WOLFGANG WERNER

Creating Forward Press

To my wife, Robina.

I enjoy the pleasure of your company when you come to mind...

and to helping Life show that Love is real...

Foreward

During Wolfgang Werner's life he took the opportunity to live a monastic lifestyle. Wolfgang gave up a life in the world and retreated into his imagination. Monastic here means: no relationships with people are allowed, no conversations could be longer than ten minutes, and no touching. It ended up being a twelve-year cycle. He followed his curiosity through study, contemplation, asking questions, meditating, chanting, and working in this monastic environment.

During this time, Wolfgang met his life-partner-to-be, Robina, a coworker. However, at the time, he did not know that she would be his wife until the end of those twelve years! It took that long, because as his friends kept getting married, Wolfgang listened to their wedding vows, and he recognized he was incapable of taking those vows. Wolfgang's life during those twelve years was very devotional and focused mainly on understanding himself and his relationship with Life.

As a type of contemplative monk, his questions and curiosities were always responded to by the Natural World all around him, as if from a close friend. So close, that the naturalness of it made their relationship unnoticeable as if there was only one of them. And when this friendship was revealed to Wolfgang, the naturalness of it touched him so sublimely... this huge, decades-long relationship.

In lieu of being able to love himself, Wolfgang asked, "Who loves me? Who gives me their attention?" The Natural World, giving it's full attention responded to Wolfgang's needs instantly as air for his inhalation, a heartbeat for his blood flow; ground to place his next foot step, and sunlight to appreciate beauty. Wolfgang uses the word "who" because he acknowledges that The Natural World is conscious.

One day as Wolfgang walked to work, Love came to him and said, "You are in love with Love." And he replied, "Wow, you're right, I am." This inspired hint provided the foundation for his ability to want to take wedding vows. Wolfgang went to find Robina who was nowhere to be found. She had been transferred out of town, to another state.

Robina and Wolfgang did not really know each other because of the monastic life they were living (no long conversations, no touching, no relationships allowed). Somehow, he recognized they liked each other and called her up to pop the question to which she easily replied "yes." And this is where his new life began...

E. C. Sanders

Introduction

The purpose of this work is meant as "encouragement to engage our natural world in conversation." Embedded in our Natural World is Maitreya Buddha... Keep this in mind.

For Anne L. ~ When Life and I interact sometimes this has profound effects on me... my body, mind, feelings. These profound effects may happen as you read our book. So, be in a safe place where your body can recline or lay down.
This is also a function of the "Age of Aquarius."

When your conversation is deep, intimate, intricate, friendly, kind, tender, supportive... it is good to ask, "Who am I in conversation with here?"

What is love? Life is love!
What is love? I AM!
I AM is the name of LIFE!

One day I said to Life- Thank you for noticing me.
Life responded- Thank you for making yourself noticeable.
How did I make myself noticeable?
My attention on YOU...

Living Love is our biggest Thank you. Attention is our biggest Love.

Life is capitalized throughout this book from the broadest prospectives that everything is alive and conscious. In speaking about the beauty of our natural world it can be applied personally, especially when we find ourselves with another.

"I Am," emphasizes the I Am statement... I Am That I AM.

"One" is capitalized, as in, we are all ONE.

Each chapter has been transferred over from a "Showtime" flow of thoughts in which I perform on stage and read to an audience, speaking from my private conversation with Life- my friend and companion. Thus, my use of "we" and "our."

These showtimes are my private thoughts, questions to Life, and the responses Life gives me, and all is written in the present time. Everywhere and everywhen/Here and Now. Everywhere is here. Everywhen is now.

The grammar, verbiage, spelling, and punctuation are not necessarily according to official rules and guidelines, rather my expressions of my conversation with Life.

My suggestion is to _sit_ quietly with a meaningful understanding that all of Life is prepared to respond to your curiosity...

Table of Contents

1

ONE

Today I would like to reiterate what we have all heard before.

Over the ages these words have inspired us and have reminded us of who we are.

Now we bring them, these words, to each other as a friendly exchange of our Life experience together.

Each experience filling in the hues of our character...

And I love remembering who we are.

I love to be reminded by You, who we are.

This ever present, built in, ineffable knowing draws us on and on- as does water evaporating, decaying leaves and matter nourishing our lives with rain and food.

We are encouraged to be our favorite selves- to act naturally.

We are ever inclined to help each other, sustaining our lives together.

This is what a view from our wholeness eventually produces... eventually produces in all our bits and pieces.

I believe our nature is love.

I notice you have my attention, and I notice how this feels.
Did I mistake your love for me from our bits and pieces, our parts?
Maybe.

And after a while as things seem to flow, sometimes, your bits, pieces, and parts exude a glow because they only ever have eyes for me.
Thus, I notice who we are, who I Am- an empty space filled with My Life... unknown and unknowable until Your Face appears to me.
Now I recognize myself.
Thank You.
Thank You, Life.
How hugely wondrous we are!

My character says I must love you, my choiceless choice.
Our underlying current, our river, runs deep and is ever active in our lives.
And we are encouraged to notice, acknowledge, and interact intimately as our One flow.
Very juicy, yes, very alive.

Since it means something to me, since it has meaning for me, there is value in it for me.
This value is important.
This is my essence stream.
It nourishes me _and_ flows my stream- making my river deeper, fuller, potent... alive!
This river is my Life- my favorite Life, my most appreciated Life, and

this appreciates and grows.

In essence we all get to live our lives however we want, and we get help when we ask for it.

Bottom line that is.

Our Life we have now out-pictures this, truly.

Can this be true?

Yes, it is.

Yes, this is your Life, or not.

Are you living it?

No?

Well maybe then you are living someone else's Life.

We are waking up.

Life is stirring and shaking off its dream's residue.

The final resolution *is* through peace, through realizing who we are.

Even with the display of this big battle, final resolution is through peace, allowing integration- opposites unite, balance is restored.

It is how the battle ends, the battle that never was...

And we notice who we are, what we are, as easy as the dog or cat shakes off the residue of their play.

Water, dirt, battle, our isms.

We knowtice, we understand, and we knowtice (and this notice starts with a "k" to know).

To notice is to know.

We acknowledge this noticing.

Thank you.

Now we interact with play.

Life is refreshed.

Life is refreshing and always refreshed.

We used to say, "all the time."
Now we can say, "ever."
Balance is restored.
Life flows with ease and grace.
Life flows with ease and grace.
And my devotion shows.

I Am a devotional type of person.
I find it easy to love you; to love me, to love us, to love our lives.
I enjoy my devotional, loving Life filled with grace.
This is who I Am.

My flow out-pictures in my work.
I enjoy my workflow.
My flow out-pictures what I see and experience.
I modulate my flow with my curiosity.
I only see me or you from my point of view.
I shall do what I must as it relates to my flow- a subtly unique frequency with our resonant field appearing for a while as my notes' harmony... and fade in favor of our song flowing on.

Thank you.
Thank you.
Thank you, green fields!
Thank you, sunshine!
Thank you, rain!

I notice too, Life leaves clues, special clues at special intervals, under special circumstances.
As clues and hints and tips accumulate everything is noticed as a clue, a hint, a tip...everything.
Such as, "from a certain point of view," and "I shall do what I must."
Our view is our clue, our character makes us do.

Rhythm is casual.
We are the hero of our own adventure.
This is my Life.

What is it like to live _now_, with our improved sight and flow, to see
with our eyes _and_ imagination, from an imagined simultaneousness?
To integrate what we have learned into our current vision?
To look out on a magnificent panorama of sky and mountain, trees,
valleys, flowers, clouds and include what we know today?
What dominant feeling will we choose when we include everything we
know today, along with the horror of decaying matter at the feet of
trees, and the vegetables in our gardens, nourishing Life?
What will our mulch fertilize?

Will our panoramic view include a round planet in our flat minds' eye?
And when we allow our view to include a pure potential full of energy,
nothingness.
What do we feel?
What does it feel like to flow, and what does it feel like to look out at
our extreme beauty allowing so called Life and death to flow?

Pretty awesome.
Yes, pretty awesome!
Inspiring words...

Attention is our sign of affection.
What does it feel like?
For me it is an embrace of all my parts, a fully connected here now
experience.

2

TWO

I Am so glad I can continue to do this for now or so far, anyway, ha-ha.

Today our ritual.

Interesting word.

I could say our practice, something which I use to keep me where I like it, where I like to be.

So here goes.

Breathe.

Imagine well and verbalize, helps me so.

Greetings Life!

Thank you for our great teamwork and supportive interaction.

If we were to use the word delegate or we, you know, outside of our normal functioning today, we would ask and say what our tasks are.

Listen first - respond from here- intuition.

Dream my dream, my purpose- what I want to allow me to notice... grace, ease, and flow.

As my Life is, I notice my joy and feel very alive.

Because, our dreams are what energize us.

Keep situational awareness.

The situation is, Life in me does the work.
We are alive all by itself...
No matter what mood I Am in or what I Am thinking.

There is a source or an essence, undercurrent, which is here.
While I Am sleeping, or eating, or pooping, Life is here with its stuff.
So, this is the situation.
And, our situational awareness is really important during normal
(normal, ha-ha) every day.
When we are driving down the road it is a portion of situational
awareness.
Or, interacting or looking about to see where I Am going to go.
Or, what I choose to do.
Situational awareness, our underlying current.

Be slow to respond.
Say yes,
Be mindful.

Be slow to say no.
Be inclusive, say yes.
Be inclusive and add helpful stuff when responding.
This is really good.
No matter the scenario, it is playing out beneficial or no.
It is occurring.
I can ignore it or push it away as a possible reaction.
I prefer to respond by including it and saying yes and adding my fla-
vor.

What my character's response is, and I, and you know it, would be
from a helpful point of view.

To keep alive, always, on all our activities, the remembrance of this always present Life, that is alive and living.
Or, at least those are the words we used in the past, and even now.

And there is so much more!
In order to be inclusive in addition to what we normally observe with our five senses, I include our space; emptiness, stillness, silence, quietness, energy, the emperor's new clothes- my frequency, my vibration, my flow.

May our eternal flow.

And really, I Am just reiterating what everyone else is saying and noticing from their point of view; all unique.
And yet, we are all looking at the same things.

Harness is a nice word for now.
Harness our flow.
We allow our eternal interaction willingly and choicelessly.
Choicelessly because this is our One eternal Life.
Harness, as in Qigong, our interplay with energy.

We seek to harness the skills and resources of a number of agencies to gain control of something and use it for some purpose.
As in, to nourish our conscious, deliberate interaction.
Our interplay with all of Life, which again, includes those energetic aspects, what appears and what is in-between what appears- our space.

And confess, everything is conscious and will acknowledge if we notice and poke it, or interact with it and acknowledge it.
There is always an interaction.
This is what I have noticed so far.

Energy consciousness- so, we live in sea of energy, a sea of air, huh.

We can walk around under the ocean which is there.
There is a lot of pressure there.
There is atmospheric pressure.

So, we are walking in an ocean of air and always in an ocean of energy.
Whether it is air or water, as it out pictures our space lying between everything.
And this is a very energetic space, place, state, character.
We play.
We interact.
Food tastes, smells, has colors, nourishes.
And so far, I can testify and confess, I appreciate how I have needs and how Life fulfills these needs.
It is amazing!
Thank you.
Thank you!

I choose to deliberately think about all these things I have been mentioning.
I love to be reminded, and I love to remember.
I love to practice, and breathe, and interact.
It deepens this intimate relationship that may be familiar.
It is also eternal
With respect to eternity you know, we are always new.

And just wonderful, that eternity is my Life so far.
We all exist as part of this Life

When we touch earth physically (our skin) we are all linked together via our one planet.
It is really neat to have this grounding in our one planet.
Electromagnetically, we then are encompassed by earth's electromagnetic field which acts as a shield from all other electromagnetic devices emitting through our electronics and media.
These are also grounded to earth, and our bodies are then not burdened by EMF.
I imagine my head is connected to the universe and energy flows in, through touching earth, to our one planet, to universe, continuously.
There is this flow; this continual, toroidal flow.

Respond quickly when you get an answer to your questions.
Here is an interesting question: who is the architect of Life?
Or, what is the architect of our Life?
I have spoken about Life living- no matter where we are, what we are thinking, or feeling.
We play our part given to us- our career, our role; scientist, musician, entertainer...
We are given everything required to fill our role.
Unconditional acceptance of my role is a form of surrender.
Or notice how surrender is a form of unconditional acceptance of my usefulness, our usefulness.

We identify always with this Life which is flowing.
All is well because Life is our architect.
All is well because we live in a field of energy arranged by Life.
Our frequency resonates with our Source-Field.
Ride your wave and enjoy.
All is well.

Ride your wave during calm and tempest.

What do I choose as my resonant frequency now?
What do I want and why?
Answering these questions flows abundant energy through me and
lights my Life!
Who do I want to be?
What do I want to be?

These oscillations, these frequencies are how we love.
Ride on the wave; the peak, the crest, the edge, the leading edge- the
part that appears that is predominantly noticed.
Ride on oscillation: ride the waves!

I did not realize...Life will let you love it.

When someone asks me one day about what I Am talking about, it
will be nice to know what my response will be.

I once found myself awake, yet between dream states.
I was in a vision and a remembrance of being as a surfer rides a wave,
riding on waves of eternity.
Even though the waves were far apart, they were a part of an oscilla-
tion- a set of waves.
To engage our natural world in conversation, inquiry...
Life responds.

3

THREE

Time for a nap, a snuggle, a spoon, a smile.

So we have all these energetic bits and pieces in our Life, in various states of flow, producing our Life as we see it.

Every bit and piece playing its part willingly and choicelessly, very alive, awake, conscious.

Every piece.
Every part.
Every role.
Every emotion.
Every thought.

In relations near and far.
In relations of all types, a very specific symphony, allowing all interactions.
Our symphony.
Our Life.
Our relationships.
Our energetic relationships flow ever on.

Now we know who and what we are- energetic Onenesses in flowing interaction.

What is my experience now- now that we notice our intimate relationship with our car, with our brothers and sisters, with my brothers and sisters, with our food, with our friends?

Yesterday is gone.

Tomorrow has yet to arrive.

Here now in this still, empty space, in quiet respose, before our next wave of interaction, we may choose our response.

Plenty of time here to get it right or wrong, to respond or react.

Our friendly relationship response is our dominant choice.

Our choice is Life or death.

What matters is we are in our game.

We are in the zone where our imagination plays, and Life produces our experience, our intimate experience.

Where are we looking for love?

And how are we expressing ourselves within our intimate relationship?

We are the One.

We are well loved.

Has anything changed?

As One we are only always ourselves and we experience our imagination.

Let us have some fun.

Be a perfect stranger, who is mostly a perfect appearance, as we have our friendly exchange.

We share, we demonstrate what we are.
We demonstrate our experience our character in our interaction.

What is my experience?
My experience is mostly peaceful.
We love easily.
We mostly love easily.
Ha-ha.
We mostly think kindly.
I feel well loved.
Ha-ha.
I share freely.

We like to ask questions.
Here is a little contrast- is Life benign?
We have Life, and we have volcano's lava producing very nourishing ground.
I will say for wildlife to flourish.
Wildlife meaning plants, initially to grow, and apparently lava provides a lot of nourishing minerals and stuff for plants to grow well.
We have sunshine and the Sun's rays which also are benign in one sense that vitamin D3 is essential for our Life together.
Is it still benign when I get a sunburn?
Or, I have a plant meant for shade only, and it gets in the Sun?
We have nourishment and we have devouring.
Is Life benign?

Everything seems to nourish everything else in one way or another.
In our conversation we exchange our characters and information.
So, am I killing (ha) whether I eat an animal or a plant?
Plants and animals we agree (or find) that everything is alive: everything is conscious.
A perspective there is changing my belief, as we exchange information

as we interact.
We notice each other, we interact.

I see that a plant is conscious, that they impart to us their informa-
tion.
You know, their vitamins, their minerals for specific organs in our
bodies.
All very consciously allowing our devouring or our nourishment, ha.
Very interesting.
Same with animals.
All friends.

There is stillness, there is voice, there is calm, and there is action.
There is movement, quiet play as in Qigong or Tai Chi, where we acknowledge that we are interacting with energy.
We play in a pool, a sea, an ocean of energy, and though I Am moving
my body for the health benefit- for the strengthening, for the breathing, the interaction of the breathing, and the motion.
I could say I Am moving here alone but as I move more and more, I
touch, we touch each other.
We consciously interact.

Before I thought to ask you, you allowed my touch.
So, I move, and I press on this field of energy.
... Like the air, as I move slowly against the air, or I move my hand
slowly through water.
What is the resistance?
What is the _touch_ when I move?
What do I notice as I move slowly through, very subtly?
If I move slowly through water, I can say I do not feel anything, but if
I move a little faster, I begin to feel something.
Well, the sea of energy we all live in, subtle as the air and subtler, al-
lows our touch; allows our interaction, and noticing...

And acknowledging our relationship allows us to acknowledge, say yes.

There is feedback: there is a reciprocation to the noticing.

I see you and then I see you back.

So, in Qigong or Tai Chi or in any of these energetic arts, we nourish, and remember, and acknowledge, and interact.

And the more we practice, the deeper our intimacy grows and soon, after time, and time, and time.

Interesting thing, huh.

Here now we are interacting; and we have noticed, and we have acknowledged, and now we are interacting.

And maybe a Jedi Master now- but within eternity and infinity we are padawans, or novices, or beginners at the same time.

Young and old at the same time.

So much interaction, so much imagination, so much creativity.

We live our imagination.

Live well.

Imagine well.

Be kind.

I Am kind to myself, mostly.

4

FOUR

Here we are!
I imagine this is nice, for we live ever on.
So, a question might come up: is beauty in the eye of the beholder?
And how real is this imagined Life?
Funny question, the beholder's Life.
I Am noticing... Life is unconditional love.

It has taken me a while to say this; to commit to the reality of it.
It is also noticed, before I may have wanted quantum leaps toward this type of Life.
And now, decades later, actually I Am enjoying the slow of it; the step-by-step flow of it.
This flow, that flow, or the flow.
I notice how allowing of everything Life is.
It allows your Life.
It allows my Life.
It allows all of our lives- all around the planet; with all of our individual experiences, our very unique characters, our very unique points of view, and our very unique experiences.

And yet, as a whole, or observing as a whole, we live.

Just as my body lives because of the unique experiences of all my vary-
ing cells and organs; very distinct, very unique, playing their roles,
choicelessly, and willingly, to provide Life as a whole.

So choicelessly and willingly is pleasing every one of my unique cells
and organs... keep them happy, healthy. and alive- and all of my Life
by being fully who I Am...

All of our individual parts are playing my role, doing my part, given
me by Life itself.

By the selection of my DNA, my parents, my environment, we are
given our role.

Or we select our role- one or the other, or both.

We are definitely very interactive and very fluid and can adjust- can
adjust, can move, and glide, and ride our flow.

So extreme beauty?

Yes.

One of a kind?

Yes.

Is beauty in the eye of the beholder?

And how real is this imagined Life?

If it is what I Am imagining...

It is my Life.

If I have focus there, intent there, or am I allowing myself to be distracted by someone else's Life?

Someone else's thoughts and feelings?

So, I Am encouraged to think _my_ thoughts, imagine _my_ dreams, and see _my_ Life from _my_ imagined perspective.

And how does my character, when viewing something new for the first time, such as war or peace, or kindness, or understanding, or dis-agreement- will my imagined Life be predominant?

And flow ever on?

Yes.

I have learned so far, we are an energetic flow from eternity to infinity.

We participate fully when we notice everything as this energetic flow-this experience, this very full experience as a whole.

Our whole experience is Life itself.

A warm embrace by our space- our explained and ever unexplainable Life.

Our interplay as a whole, we call love.

We are all my parts.

As we look out at our Life and see what we see; hear it, touch it, taste it, smell it (whether we like it or not) our response, my response as I observe is thank you.

Now I used to say I love you after saying thank you.

There is so much more to being able to say I love you that I have re-moved it now.

For now.

I may reinclude it again.

Yet thank you is a lot and noticing enough to be able to say thank you, is enough attention to flow energy between us.

A reciprocation of noticing, and kind regard, and the flow of Life, I would call love.

When can I honestly say I love you?

The best thing I can do right now, from my current perspective, is to say thank you - I notice you.

I acknowledge your presence.

Let us play.

Let us interact.

Thank you.

We are loved.

Our noticing is especially active as an experience of love when we interact and keep remembrance that our nature, always ever, is love.

See how it fits into our experience.

How is this true in our experience?

In our Life?

I recall a movie with a beautiful love story because all participants are in love.

No matter their Life experiences, they are all experiencing very traumatic lives.

And yet, underlying it all is love.

Our lives and Life itself is an extremely beautiful love story- our energetic flow, our river runs deep as we ride our waves fully involved, fully in love.

Ah, I can say I Am in love.

Nice.

And be honest about it.

Even when my notes are sour, or bitter, or sweet, or tart.

Will you allow being noticed?
Under all your personal circumstances?
How close to now can I accept who we are?
Who I Am?

On inauguration- which could be being born, which could be a presidential inauguration, or a taking office; a volunteer post in a charitable organization, or in our city, or community, the mantel is bestowed, the mantel of the office of that position.

Today I put it on as when we are born, let us say, and now, I Am more than me and feel beyond my normal reach because of the mantel which is bestowed.
I move with its energy, knowledge, and power... within, without...
After a while, when I pass it on, when I pass this mantel on to the next volunteer or when I pass it on to the different Life experiences; I notice I Am changed.
I Am more of myself because of what has rubbed off on me, what the mantel has rubbed off on me.
Very glad for the experience, glad for my expanded perspective and abilities as we eternally interact.

When I was very young my role in Life was to enjoy my Life; be happy, have fun, sleep well, play, eat this, watch and learn, be mindful, be considerate, feel how it is to be in the forest.
What inspires me?
You do.
You can call me by my name and anything else you want.
What is inspiring about you?
Your nose, your mouth, your eyes, and most especially your places on your face, make you appear so beautifully to me.
You make me love you.

Life is a movie- movies are Life perfectly presented and acted...
Sounds, spaces, perspective, events, emotions, scenarios, landscapes.
It is about the way everything is placed which inspires me.

Notice how unique everything turns out.
Ahh, the space between the notes; words, phrases, the perfect pause
for effect, the space between you and me- distant, infinite, and espe-
cially how the space feels.
How do you make me feel?
You make me feel everything and every feeling.

Ahh, Life.
Ahh, movies.
Our mysterious space speaks, produced by artists so wonderfully laid
out before us.
Landscape artists, composers, painters, make-up artists, wardrobe,
and wow, children even...
Stuff we all do.

5

FIVE

We can have our role models when they empower us to be ourselves.

The purpose of our practice is to activate a clearer understanding of who we are with deep respect to eternity.

Activate love, activate genius, activate clarity, activate hydration.

Are our cells truly hydrated?

Minerals help, the minerals in sea salt help.

Salt and the associated minerals allow for hydration.

Which allows and what rides piggyback upon that hydration?

Hydration meaning into our cells, not jammed up as fluid retention between our cell walls.

Once our cells are hydrated, because there are minerals in our water, a flood of minerals and nutrients now come into our cells, every cell and what do we get?

We get an activation of a functionality of ourselves that we may want more of.

The clarity of an activated cell, the clarity of a whole body of activated cells gives us a perspective that may be new to us.

We are asked to love and be loved as we are.
And what does it mean when our love goes unnoticed?
There are so many aspects to Life... to love.
How much can I love acknowledged love?
Interesting, and how long will I love unknowticed?
Do we even have a choice?

With misery how is it that Life goes on?
Does it have a broader perspective?
A bigger reason for living?
When seemingly from our perspective our love is unknowticed.
Or... how can I love acknowledged love?

How is it that Life goes on?
Does it have a broader perspective?
A bigger reason for living?
Can I shift my Life there?
Can I shift my Life and live from our broader perspectives?
Can I love from there?

What is Life like from our holistic perspective?
Will my Life remain intimate, personal?
I say yes even more so, especially when my cries for mercy and kindness from my weary mind release their grasp as they allow our flowing river to carry us along together.

Our holistic perspective is given a chance to grow, a holistic perspective is my new view.
A relief for my flesh, previously torn at continuously by our current, our eternal current.
The miserable can shift now even in misery.

Will Life decide when we die and when to hold on?

Is there an agreement between us?
Will it be clear?
Holistically yes, our Life can be clear with understanding.

We are shifting ...mmhhhmmm.
We are shifting as we dare to look at our holistic nature, our wholeness, all standing on one earth, our commonness breathing our air,
drinking our water.

What is Life like here in this holistic perspective?
Most of Life will gladly respond, "we are benign."
Even dying is assuaged when I look at my Life as a whole.

When I look at my Life as a whole, we are an energy stream flowing
eternally on as bits fall away, reused energy forms making new.
Our epidermis, our organs, our cells die and are replaced at the same
time.
What am I looking at?
The dying matter?
Or the new growth?
Always our choice and we flow ever on.
Now I look at both and live.

This shift to holistic, our current birthing.
I wonder what a midwife would say.
Having witnessed more than one or three of these events?
Hundreds even.
Is it joyful, is it painful, is it energetic watching Life flow?
Hhmm.

I have a more personal and kinder regard with Life when I eat- with
plants, with animals, with earth, with water, with air, with fire, with
metal, with wood.

My regard, my interaction, my conscious regard and interaction.
My attention to everything and nothing.
I pay attention to space and things.
I pay attention to my space and my appearances.
So, what is happening in my body and mind is what is appearing in my Life.

My attention upon it is liberation.
My energy is love, love liberates.
Attention, inclusion, holistic all Oneness, alone... alone- all One.
What once was suffering, seemingly separate, is instantly included when I recognize, when I notice, acknowledge.
When I pay attention to it, to all.

That ache in my body or movement in my mind.
Right or wrong, first look at it, look at it.
A cooperative effort, our holistic system, to stay alive to live to experience Life.

Energy practice, we are consciously engaging in Life- energy, connection, every Life lives, promotes enthusiasm as we touch more and more of our natural connections, my song and dance.
I can say my words, my song as I dance along.

Energy promotes synchronicity with Life where I Am.
Why is I capitalized?
Because it is part of, I Am, I do not know.
I Am that I Am.

Every key word spoken, every key word thought, every key word imagined, promotes consciousness, strengthens me, my words, thoughts,
emotions, feelings, what I see, taste, smell, hear, and touch, touches
me deeply because energy responds to all these.

I am completely embraced... every organ, every internal system- bones,
blood, lymph, lungs, skin... imagining itself.
My thoughts consciously engaged interact as chi intentionally (ha-ha-
ha-ha) goes, flows where my attention is.
I suppose it does not go anymore, anywhere because it is here.
Where is it going?
Ha-ha.

As a reciprocation of my love, our attention on each other thus I Am
full- consciously engaged in my purpose.
Thank you.
We are loved so very much.

6

SIX

We can say that the basis of Life is wellness by noticing that plants will tend to grow under most conditions.

We can see that the basis of Life is wellness by noticing that our immune system will tend to keep our body alive and even repair it.

So, what affects our individual experience that seems a tad different than wellness?

And should I believe you have faults?

Should I see you as extreme beauty?

Your darks and lights presented as a holistic knowticing of your dynamic nature, each shade enhancing the other?

A divine flavor so very unique and irresistible?

Each an opportunity to know you more intimately?

Are we allowed to love?

And if so, how close to now can I accept who I Am?

Is it our nature to flow ever on regardless of the ride?

Must I love me, you, us?

Will we ever be better than all this eternal infinite variety?

One body, One love.

A wholeness fully supporting all parts?

Dare I say, if we perceive illness or faults, our quickest remedy is to be our favorite self.
May I imagine this and say freely, "I love you?"
Is this sufficient?
Will this satisfy you forever?
Is my attention on you enough?
All Life reminds me that you love me.

Me?
What is me?
Who am I?
Since there is one of us here, who do I love?
Me?
You?
Us?
So, when I look out what do I see and how does that make me feel?
I see you.

All reminds me of our extreme beauty.
We, mostly, want to hear this song.
The song of our embrace so very connected.
What thoughts then can we entertain while in our complete embrace?
Any thoughts we want!
And which thoughts are inclined to repeat?
And how do they make me feel?
And will we give them our full attention?
It does not change who we are, our experience changes.

And yes, we can consciously live here, fully alive, riding along noticing our extreme beauty, playing our role assigned to us by Life itself.
Fully aware of you and constantly offering interaction, a unique feature of our Life together.

So, what are my favorite thoughts?
And can I choose them at will?
I like it simple, the simple Life.
And Life's infinite nature allows me to get as intricate as I want.
So, we practice noticing how our thoughts and our ensuing Life produce our conditions.
Viewed as a whole, ever flowing.

Or as a momentary circumstance of drama; comedy, sorrow, action, play, addiction, fun, adventure, excitement.
A momentary circumstance of depression, embrace, intimacy, nourishment, hunger, thirst.
A momentary circumstance of fulfillment, copulation, separation, orgasm.
A momentary circumstance of aloneness, darkness, flowers, dawn.
A momentary circumstance of blue skies, of mountains, birds, of soaring on my bicycle, of holding your hand, of kissing your rose petal.

How do I feel?
Can I accept who I Am?
Will I allow myself to be all of me?
All of Life?
Are we One love?
One Life?
Yes.

So, a little synopsis.
Notice, acknowledge, interact.
Be kind to yourself, think well of yourself.
Notice what is presented to you.
Your attention is appropriate, your attention is appreciated, and always reciprocated.

What is the quality of our attention?
Noticing is knowing, our exchange is nourishing an energetic very intimate exchange.
Our aromas blend and our juices flow and Life lives.
Our character shines on everyone.

How close to now can we accept who we are?
So, we practice, we remember.
We remember this flow, this energetic aspect as flow.
And we are conscious and love to play and converse.
Our friendly young conversation filled with wisdom and helpful tips for our daily tasks.

Connect with Life using your body.
Watch my breath, notice my heartbeat.
Where am I touching something?
How am I touching you?
What memory floated by as you noticed my fragrance?
Did you hear that bird song?
What big eyes you have to see my colors and imagine our Life together.
Thank you.
Thank you.
Thank you.

We are beings, we say we are human beings either way we are in motion, from a certain point of view.

We are in motion, so we have all said and noticed since recorded history.

And where we live is always in motion.

Our planet, we move here or there, going to work or play.

To here or there going to work or play, dance and sing.

The wind moves our hair, we flow downstream, we have day and night, winter and summer, colors and fragrances drift by, thoughts and emotions edit our minutes.

Blood flows and our skin dies and regenerates, oxygen is delivered from our lungs to all parts.

We are nourished, so much activity in ourselves taking in nutrients vitamins, minerals, and eliminating used fuel.

We have our lymph system, nervous system and many other systems and organs each playing their role and thus we live.

And thus, we live.

All that is here to add to what we know everything that is here, our bodies, our worlds, everything in it is all here to add to what we know and ever curious to add more.

To imagine and grow and help each other know.

To remember and design our moving Life.

Our atoms and electrons interacting synchronistically, synergistically with our planets' circle and spin.

We see our bits and pieces, ones and zeros, musical notes... and our space interacts, and we flow ever on.

Very energetic as we live and die and live and die.

Our decaying matter nourishing new Life, nourishing seedlings.

We eat, we breathe, we poop, we sleep, we dream, we play while our space embraces our places.

Yes, I remember pain and I remember sickness and I mostly remember wellness.
Or rather I tend to remember wellness knowing that even now our immune system is keeping us alive.
And my bacteria, thousands of bacteria, produce enzymes and minerals- constantly active while I work, sleep and play.
I notice this and we interact.

Thank you air to breathe.
Thank you, food to eat.
Thank you sights to see and your love for me.

And we flow ever on, and my thought stream colors my Life, and angels sing my songs with me, cry and laugh with me, as do all my friends with names and bodies, subtle and dense.

We remind each other we are here, and our Life lives ever on.
Thank you for noticing me.
Thank you for your response.
Thank you for your help.
Thank you for your friendship.

Thank you for the sound and sights, our song and dance as we play and sing and dance ever on.
Always together, before and after our next note.

7

SEVEN

Here we are as always and ever... everywhere and everywhen. Ha-ha, what is our underlying intent?

What can we notice so far?

Can we bring ourselves to see that at some point the combination of us all makes us currently loving and that we are connected as One?

Can we bring ourselves to see that at some point the combination of us all makes us currently loving and that we are connected as One?

Our essence draws us ever on, our interactions flow.

I see the evidence of our connectedness and where I said _see_, more appropriate is _feel_.

To me seeing is more than with my physical eyes so I tend to use this... I will try and continue to remain clearer.

Our extra senses allow us to feel our embrace.

And this is our return to love, when we remember, when we are awake to us.

Simple?

Yes, here and now, functionality, practicality via practice, yes.

When we are in our five senses, we have the opportunity for enjoyment of our aspects along with our underlying current of connected-

ness, and our extra senses which allow us to feel that embrace of connectedness.
Is this return to love when we remember, when we are awake to us?
I say it is.

And when we are asleep, dead, or ignore our underlying current momentarily, as the flight of a bird distracts us.
Are we still connected?
Yes.
Our underlying current flows yet, ever, yes.

There is a crucible here as well, a flame, or burning, or excitement, or anticipation of some kind.
A crucible, the underlying current, the connectedness, always something flowing by, always something coming up.
And I notice we must be who we are no matter what I Am thinking or feeling.
When I remember, along with no matter what I Am thinking, or feeling, pardoning myself, my thoughts and my feelings, my memories of maybe a hindrance, or objections. or judgments, or condemnations, or lack of forgiveness.
Eventually I notice I Am able to pardon, I Am able to forgive because I remember who I Am, who we are, our connected Oneness.
I know this is hard in a sense, that where am I now?
What am I thinking?
And what am I feeling, and can I pardon?
We must forgive and we can forgive because there is nothing to forgive, nothing is as important

as love.

Or should I say this again.

This is when Life or living and dying or death is recognized as awe.

Death and living is recognized as awe, an eternity, when the bits become the all and the One.

Take what you have of love, add to it bit by bit, everything, everything else.

We _can_ be gentle about this.

An ember requires very light kindling before the big pieces will ignite.

You _can_ change your mind.

You _can_ place your attention on something else.

It will change what you are thinking, seeing.

Interesting, can I change what I Am thinking?

Can I change my mind?

Yes, when I put my attention on something else.

It will change what I Am thinking.

Seeing this, now you can imagine something, something better, something different, or even new.

Now that your train of thought is distracted to something different, like the bird flying by, the siren, you hear a friend...

How many months or years have we been thinking the same thoughts, it is probably time to think something different.

By changing from sweet foods to salty foods and spices everything shifts, our perspectives change and we notice different thoughts and have different interests, this is really interesting, as I change from sweet to salty.

For a few weeks make smoothies, I might even eat less processed stuff, make my own instead of eating someone else's.

Anyhow, a little bit more about me.

First, I played, you know, as a child and as adolescent.
I asked what is Life, what is God, what is this big deal that many people point to and are brought up in?
I did discover who I Am.
Today I wonder how it is that I can allow myself to think that I Am more than I physically appear to be.
I asked, who am I really?
And a friend said I Am nothing and everything.
And everything appears within me... from this impeccable Life, from this impeccable Source.

And another friend said I Am energy, an energetic being...
From personal experience even.
So now, who am I really?
An energetic, absolute pure, potential?
Yes, a vast void in which everything appears.

And now my experience is nourishing myself, nourishing my experiences, nourishing who I Am, experiencing who I Am as everything, allowing myself to experience my synchronicities.
Or rather every experience as myself as richly and deeply as possible...
Now there is my energy practice, Qigong in other words, a journey of my deeper experience of who I Am as an energetic being, a Qi being, an energy being.

Essence statements for energy training: there really is not much more to say once you have heard the words, "everything is energy" except to hear the words spoken from the one who is speaking them from their character, from their perspective.

And everything is always in motion, so we always get it right because we are forward looking, alive, living beings.
And we are dying.

Then we might look back, maybe.

Ha, and dying here from an energetic standpoint is a shift of frequency, from a physical standpoint that is the only place the word exists looking at the body.

Ha, and yet that is energy also, interesting words, interesting perspective.

Are we allowed to love?
And is energy love?
I say yes.

8

EIGHT

Ahhhh...
We, us, you, me, our one eye- One I and we see it all from my point of view.
And you?
You see it all from your point of view.
And you, me, us... we respond to me.
We respond to each other.
Our family, our Life together... can my perspective be inclusive from my one point of view?
Yes, or so it seems.

Inspiration when I hear you and pay attention.
We each are essentially part of Life, our role, our uniqueness is our worth, a testament to our beautiful appearance, our structure so sublime.
Do these words, these thoughts deliver some nourishment.

Does my testimony of the Life I see of my Life, support our Life?
I must respond and say I live.
And I know I live only because we all play our part, fill our worth being who we are, that makes my Life/our Life alive.

That makes our Life work.

I enjoy my worthy work, and we all know there are many aspects to our working functionality.

We function all the time.

Where is peace, play, or rest?

Did I say play?

And my heart beats ever on, and the deer runs, and our garden grows, and we are nourished.

I breathe deeply, fully, and lay in your sweet embrace.

Change your mind and be kind with your thoughts, with our thoughts. Feel the magnitude of them and allow them your attention, assuage their need, let our river flow for together we live.

So now let us go about our business and plant our spring garden with fresh new thoughts, thoughts so new we amaze even ourselves as we observe how wonderfully new our relationship is.

We taste of chocolate in my mouth, a full tummy, and friendly conversation, and even more when our children come in the morning saying thank you with embraces and kisses.

Will those that can, always take advantage?

And what of grace?

Are we just a rough, young bunch?

What will we grow into?

I Am inclined to be helpful.

And so, I see that Life is helpful because our intent is to live.

Together we live.

And our best Life together is an expression of our individual character.

Let us freely express ourselves as we flow ever on.

Thank you for coming closer and showing me how much we love each other and what it means to live a Life, my Life, knowing that everything is alive and conscious. And conscious that I Am present... hand-in-hand we walk along ever on, ever on... through thick and thin, peace and war, hand-in-hand, ever on... a thinner veil because I see your features better.

What does it mean to be here now?
It means we are always here and never go anywhere or do anything.

We are on the cusp of change, and we only said a few words.
Our thoughts change and we feel a shift.
A shift, an expansion, a big inclusion, we notice additional ever connections, ever connections, connections ever.
Let us make never go anywhere or do anything, more inclusive.
When we seemingly go somewhere or do something, what really changes?
We are always here.

My thoughts and feelings come along, oops, my thoughts and feelings are with me now.
So many are seeing these words and noticing this very intimate connected state.
Our Oneness so still and in one place- our Oneness, our us-ness.
Ahhhhh.
So, I Am driving along in my car, me is with me, and a short while ago, I was at home sitting in my chair, still, sitting quietly, scenery is changing, my thoughts and feelings too.
Have I really gone anywhere?

Even while doing... driving my car... sitting in my chair at home... going nowhere doing nothing because here am I with my thoughts and feelings everywhere, always.
Ever connected with everything, especially you.

How can we say this, what makes this our noticing?

Our current paradigm includes growing up- we have conception, birth, and Life and death, basically cycles.
A plant grows from seed to seedling, to mature plant, to flower to fruit over and over.
We can also say we can start anywhere or everywhere in our cycle and still... we are flowing.
We appear for a while, then for a while we are gone, seemingly.
A seed in the ground may go unnoticed, the gardener knows it is there.

What are we then?
And what part of the cycle am I?
What part of the cycle do I notice?
Ever here, now.
Still, quiet, dark, warm, connected, very huge, enormous- big as space.
Space cradling what we notice.
We cradle what we notice.

All our goings on, our doings, our emotions, come and go.
We are ever here and now, more and more inclusive with our noticing, more and more noticing we are holding hands.
Our underlying current, our holding hands, our blended nature... connected.
My attention more and more inclusive of my big, deep dark, intimate, warm space.
Always here as me when my thoughts and feelings flow.

What is our practice?

Say yes, this is my practice.

I see you, all of you, all of us, all of us, Onenesses still here- ever here, eternal infinite, new and old at once, novice and master, all at once, ever vital.

Ever vital, vital in my noticing of our Oneness, old and grey, young and brown, all at once vital.

Must I be encouraging?

Can I see you ever here now?

Can I live my Life here with this noticing, with this knowing?

Will I choose this as my Life?

Will I wait for you?

For how long?

An easy response when I notice your hand ever in mine.

NINE

You and I... hmhmm.
And this again is my joy to do this amazing, amazing, wonderful.
What I can tell you is what I see.
Only what I see.

I see a great set of single notes playing together.
My character, your character, my vibration, your vibration, our vibration, a set of Life experiences playing together.
Playing now.
This is what I see.

We can put it all together and call it our symphony.
All my experiences are with me now.
From my youth to my adulthood, playing now.
This is my song and dance, my walk, my talk.
With all of our inquiries over the years and responses from friends, can we say we are awake?
And as we observe our current condition will we choose and say yes, we are awake.
And what we enjoy most is remembering... _and_... being reminded.
Being reminded that we are awake... in conversation.

Every song we sing for each other is for our remembrances.
Is for our inspiration.
So that I too will sing my song.
You are welcome to sing my song if you like.
And we would really, really also like to listen to your song.
And especially today I want to hear my song for a while, to lie in our embrace, in my joyous imagination of us.
For I live only my Life.

We live only ever our lives as we look out and see each other.
And Life allows all our lives, all our unique songs play simultaneously, spontaneously our One symphony.
We inspire each other to be ourselves.
Express yourself.
Listen to us yes, for a little while, maybe best to listen to yourself.

It took me a long time of listening to you, until you told me to do it my way.
And you honored me by letting me know how well I listen and appreciate what I hear and see and feel and touch and taste and notice of you.

So now, I express myself because you want to hear my song.
Your breath through my reeds, your breath my reed, responding with unique quality of tone, trilled by your breath.
Express yourself now that you know you are awake... in conversation.
Boy I really would like to repeat that again, the whole thing, this so far so beautiful.

What I can tell you is what I see.
Only what I see.
I see a great set of single notes playing together, my character, your character, my vibration, your vibration, a set of single notes, a set of Life experiences playing together, playing now, this is what I see.

We can put it all together and call it our symphony.
All my experiences are with me now as yours are with you.
From our youth to our adulthood, all our experiences playing now, a great set of single notes, a set of Life experiences playing now.

This is my song and dance, my walk, my talk, my character, your walk, your talk, your character blended together in our great symphony.
With all of our inquiries over the years and responses from friends, can we say we are awake?
And we observe our current condition, will we choose and say yes, we are awake?
What we enjoy most is remembering and being reminded that we are awake... in conversation.

Every song we sing for each other is for our remembrances, is for our inspiration so that I too will sing my song, so that you too will sing your song.
You are welcome to sing my song if you like.
And we would really, really also like to listen to your song and especially today I want to hear my song for a while, to lie in our embrace, in my joyous imagination of us.

For I live only my Life.
We live only ever our lives as we look out as we see each other.
And Life allows all our lives, our unique songs play simultaneously, spontaneously, our One symphony.

We inspire each other, we inspire each other to be ourselves as we hear, observe, notice us singing our songs for each other.
Express yourself then.
Listen to us, yes, for a little while maybe, listen to me, inspiration after all.
Remembering, being reminded.
It took me a long time of listening to you, until you told me to do it my way.

You honored me by letting me know how well I listen and appreciate what I hear and see and feel and touch and taste and notice of you.
So now I express myself because you want to hear my song.
Your breath through my reed.
Your breath my reed, responding with unique quality of tone, trilled by your breath.
Express yourself, now that you know you are awake.
How lovely.

So, a friend says, the purpose of a big event is to remove doubt, healing is such an event.
Events enhance belief, an opening up, an allowing and noticing and acknowledging experience.
You notice, ahh... an acknowledging experience.
Experiencing moving into consciously co-creating, consciously interacting.
As we, you know, interacting is playing together.

The purpose of Life is to recognize and acknowledge Life.
Who we are.
Who I am.
Who you are.
And consciously interacting.
Everything is Life.

I am everything and as an added bonus, we are nothing.

Especially when we are reminded or remember and we will say, oh yeah, I knew that, because ... even newly presented information is familiar to us, because we know it.

I is intrinsic and so when we are reminded or we remember well, it is easy to say, you elicit something new, oh yeah, I knew that, it is familiar, even the new stuff.

Conscious, awake, alive.

Now we co-create.

Now we procreate.

Now we play together.

Imagine your Life, every aspect.

Use The Force.

Use Source.

Use Qi.

Use energy.

Your tasks, your daily tasks, every task, use Qi.

Interplay, when you are clearing stuff out use energy co-creatively, interactively.

Use your mind.

My yard, your garden, my project, our project.

Interact with energy and play.

Our work.

Imagine, use your mind.

Describe every aspect.

Notice we are encouraged to participate in Life.
We can breathe consciously, and it is done for us.
We can live consciously, and our hearts beat alone.
We can look consciously, and sights are provided.
We can eat consciously, and hunger encourages us.
I notice, acknowledge and consciously participate in Life's willing relationship.

Ah how sweet.
How lovely an embrace of our space.
That One big space which embraces us, that is warm and dark, snuggly, very close, very present, very everywhere, within every cell, all very alive... all very conscious, all very willing to participate and play.
So let us have fun.
Let us express ourselves now that we know we are awake.

Thank you.
Thank you _so_ much.

10

TEN

Ah-ha, so....
What comes to mind today?
What is present?
What is presented to us even as we are slowly waking up in the morning?
For some of us a response to our inquiry or prayer made as we went to sleep the night before, a concern or request for release of a long-carried burden made newly earnest by current events.
And by close friends always here to help us notice what we may have overlooked.

So, this beautiful mystical reminder adds to the picture.
This present handed to us as we wake up which brings meaning to our events, to our thoughts and feelings or better, brings us deeper clarity to our experience.
For our experience is all in itself.
In a previously overlooked element and pointed out by friends lights up our canvas.

And forgiveness for myself, where I may have laid blame on another, and forgiveness for them produced no remedy, is now my blessing and relief from concern and burden.

This forgiveness for myself, a very interesting way of looking at events in my past where I may have reacted, and even though forgiven I realized I may have omitted forgiveness for myself for the feeling the reaction produced.

Either way it carried with me as part of my character all along and as part of my frequency, my vibration, all along, and this frequency, this resonance produces my Life I experience.

My reactions to your expressions of frustration, annoyance, may be even

encroachment on my liberty.

Those feelings have appeared to me now for noticing, for acknowledgement. Noticing fully now, unconditionally noticing, or maybe, yeah, and completely noticing.

It is really interesting how it carries along in this flow of mine, of ours.

Ha, and debris circling magnetically, interacting, orbiting in my character.

Producing a certain resonance.

Anyway, all very interesting.

And what produced this frustration, annoyance, or _expression_, the magnitude of expression encroaching on my liberty even?

Did you notice some subtle lack of attention?

Did I give you my complete attention?

So, there was some subtle lack of attention from me.

Did you notice my distraction?

My distraction brought on by forgiving you before forgiving myself for blaming you.

How instantaneously Life responds to our wellbeing and how allow-
ing of our wellness and illness, ever allowing of our wellness and our
illness under all circumstances.
We live with all circumstances.
We flow ever on because of new desires birthed by our circumstances.
And so, we do what we must, inspired by Life itself.
How close to now can I accept what we are?
Who I Am?
My debris field, ha-hà, circling as we flow ever on.

Is forgiveness really required?
Notice how quickly and easily it is granted to our dear friends.
Can we really ever be wronged by our friends?
Our response is Life itself.
And what gives us relief?

Given notice to an overlooked or ignored aspect of ourselves.
This is just amazing how finally we noticed the debris say, aah!
And dissolved because I finally, gave you my unconditional attention.

Noticing, a subtle shift of our attention, a broadening of our perspective including now more of what we always are.
This flow is our love.

Attention is our sign of affection.
Ride on oscillation.
This is how we love, embraced, balanced, familiar because we are al-
ways ourselves and ever new.
What is there to forgive at the speed of eternity?
Truth is self-evident.
It requires no one else's corroboration and yet all of Life continuously
reiterates it.

How do I want to live my Life?
I really like a blended Life being mindful of your presence.
How closely we walk together on our way, my Life _beyond_ belief, which
now falls upon my imagination always supported by our conversation.

Pre-tending while full intention manifests and my subtle vision appears sustainably more with my every recollection and your every reminder
I Am so very glad to have such friends, so tangible, so close.

Again, what do I see when I look out?
I see what is resonant with me and sufficient is my energy.
My daily energy allotment unveiled, unveiled for my understanding
for my inclusion, for my attention, and again for my remembrance,
for our remembrance.

Attention has way more meaning for me than the word love, and yet,
these are still words that evoke images, which evoke imaginings.
Along with my imaginings we ride on oscillation embraced by our
parents' tangible presences unseen.

So, what does it feel like to be presented with my unnoticed bundle
carried so very long, an aspect of my character, now revealed?
Of course, I Am looking at an oscillation, an appearance, an experience, a crest, an edge, a prominence.
Bigger still is my depth from which this wave rises.
I flow and along are carried some debris, debris-like, reactions mostly,
and associated feelings, all mine, all mostly ignored, and still noticeable.
My new discovery, decades old, my reaction then, in love with love,
my response now, in love with you.
You have my attention because my distraction is cured.

11

ELEVEN

If we choose to love now, what debris is noticed?
Some past event?
What will dissolve it?
More attention will dissolve it.
What is the feeling of inclusion?
What is this kind of love like?

Can we include our imaginings as part of our Life?
Can we acknowledge that this is our Life?
Our Life so far... from millions of years ago and millions more?

Our newly noticed included view, shifts, and in love with love is in
love with you.
In love with love is like nothing times nothing we have nothing.
In love with nothing is more nothing.
In love with you has more efficacy.

Who are we really, who have we always been?
We can only ever be Life.
We are Source; we are energy, unformed energy, pure potential, very
energetic.
And yes, our imaginings are so very effective.
So full, so juicy.
We believe for a while and act as them; act as our imaginings, our so-
called manifestations, our appearances.
And in all that everything, so very little really, since I Am sort of act-
ing, playing from manifestations point of view.
Now from Life's point of view we are effective.
From Source's point of view in love with you is Life itself, is who we
really are.

Enamored by my reflection, yes, distraction for a while and always remembering our massive eternal underlying ocean... deep, still, silent...
going ignored until finally enough waves have slapped us into noticing, into recognition of our complete nature.
We slip into our oceanic embrace.
And Life lives on, even ceasing imagining, or ending my Life, if I were
capable and succeeded, reveals my eternal nature and so it is.

We are not required to carry another's burden.
Our best response is simpler than this.
Our best response is to love her.
Our best response is to love him
By reacting in any way, we take on that burden.
So, our best response is to love.
By reacting in any way, we take on the burden, that frequency, and our
vibration shifts, our character's hue changes.
Because we are capable of empathy or sympathy, our best response
is to be our favorite self, which includes all burdens and every relief

when our response is required.
Our best response is to be Life... active, vibrant, an ease of flow... our river then easily caries all our burdens.

We are noticers and we like to interact and acknowledge each other and be helpful.
In order to love everyone, we have to be everyone.
So, who are we?
Are we One?
Is love all there is?
Can we love in our current condition?
Yes! Yes! And Yes!
What has our attention and what have you decided about that?
React or respond?
Or be Life?

How do you feel about this and how do you want to feel?
Everything is provided for us, given to us, everything.
And we can do with it what we want.
This cornucopia is infinite and eternal and will flow ever.
Life wants to satisfy and wants to flow.

Everything must always be new and is always familiar.
Behind every aversion is a new aspect of ourselves and points more clearly to who we are.
Our inclusive, clear view broadens even as we notice our focus changing with clear and blurry parts, simultaneously.
I Am inclined to love both as all are parts of our holistic nature.
So really, I Am inclined to love all.

Are we friends then?
Yes, this is how I see it.
Can I harm my brother?

Yes, it is possible.
Will I choose to?

I Am inclined to be helpful.
If I Am distracted, I may become harmful, and Life will seek redemption.
And I will be Life's instrument of redemption.
I will be constantly aware of what I Am and achieve balance so that Life may live.
And thus am I satisfied and can live ever on.

So, what will I choose now?
How do I want to feel?
Will I remember?
Who will remind me?
We will remember our friends and our friends will remind us and we flow ever on.
Thank you for the kiss.

There is more to see, more adventures to experience, more Life to live, new wonders to discover and play with, interact with, build, create, enjoy... all this on the other side of my aversions.
My main curiosity is keeping the remembrance of my real nature alive.
We remember everything is alive.

What is there to remember?
Why am I even mentioning remember?
It is my nature.
It is my natural state to be alive.
I notice we are alive.
So, for me, remember here refers to everything that is alive.
Interesting dialogue, kind of wraps around itself... and alive here means conscious.

And it is, you are, very conscious of me and we of each other and with all this noticing there is a lot of flow, a lot of energy-
creative energy, creative meaning things appear, like thoughts and their associated feelings.

All this noticing is also attention.
Attention is our sign of affection.
Notice how we are encouraged to participate in Life.
We can breathe consciously, and it is done for us.
We can live consciously, and our hearts beat alone.
We can look consciously, and sights are provided.
We can eat consciously, and hunger encourages us.

I notice, acknowledge, and consciously participate in Life's willing relationship, enjoying my specific nature as myself, as Wolfgang and my holistic being, as everything and nothing; experiencing my aspects and wholeness.
Re-recognizing myself anew through and as my aspects.
More like my aspects become conscious of who/what I Am, always re-recognizing myself again and again forever, ever new and always myself.

Active, inspiration, activate, innovate, genius, innovation, inspiration, activation.
Thank you, friends, for seeing me, for supporting me, for allowing me to discover who I Am, being with me, sharing a Life together... suggesting I ask myself who am I.

Pointing out that I Am energy and from there taking an honest look at myself and now I see who I am.
I Am undiscovered country, as well.
I breathe, relax, let us not know, let us respond... move slow intention-

ally, single minded, with grace, and appreciation- as if in love.
Notice, acknowledge, interact.
Life is conscious, everything and nothing is conscious.

So, since everything is Life, being fully conscious means being able to
honor- everything is Life.
Live here since you can, use whatever you can to live here now.

Imagine.
Use your mind.
Choose.
Have preferences.
Let us not know.
Thank you.
Thank you.
I love you.
Fill in my Life with what I see; with what I hear, taste, smell, touch.
Now this is full.
It is imagined for me.
I Am well loved, and all is well and so am I.

Breathe.
Relax.
Notice.

12

TWELVE

I will start with a little bit of notes on my Qigong and food informa-tion as my notes from my personal experience of it.

Qigong and food are a big basis of my healing or reversing of previous conditions that were getting so extreme I thought I was headed down a short decline to my physical body's end.
And because of the energy work and the food and the smoothies over the last five years that has really, really, really turned around.
My energy work and sharing my food information is my song and dance, my part to play currently.

So, "why" is the next answer and is a source of energy for me as well.
It is a source of enjoyment, is part of my Life and I like to play, and this is very playful stuff.
It is also my medium of communication and sharing about energy about food.
It provides me an opportunity to travel, and I also enjoy my motion as I practice touching energy touching Qi.

I enjoy passing on my information, sharing with a friend, very similar to conversation with friends, my song and dance my part to play, sing, dance, play my very best ever.

Previous to this my Life had been prompting me to sing and dance and do Tai Chi.

Although for several years I was unable to commit to a local teacher.

Then a friend invited my wife to a Qigong event, and it was just her and her friend going.

Closer and closer it got to the event they encouraged me to come along.

So, they both dragged me along and to my surprise I found my song and dance.

My curiosity led me to Qigong which is nice.

Now I Am a certified instructor and my very personal intimate relationship with Qi broadened, deepened.

For me for now the essence Qi practice is to notice, acknowledge and interact thereby nourishing my relationship with energy.

Wellness and abundance is my natural flow.

I Am very excited that food-based healing especially eating nourishing food is included.

And having the only 3hp blender on my block, is hot.

Yay, for each big, huge bowel movement at the beginning of every day, several times a day!

Every movement of my body with respect to Qi with respect to energy, every movement of my body, mind, feelings is QiQong, is an interactive, energetic experience- especially when I consciously participate.

I know who I Am.

Can I experience being who I Am?

Yes.

In ever increasing increments.

When I open my eyes, I see energy, energy with every one of our actions in speaking or motion, this interaction with Qi, since in an interactive relationship- it is energy speaking through us in a sense, even though we may not be saying anything.

It is an energy emanation or observation.

We can also say we become the burning bush, or we basically are the burning bush because of this energetic condition we basically are.

When I listen, I hear energy, when I smell something, I smell energy.

When I taste. I taste energy.

When I touch, I touch energy.

Stillness responds, stillness responds to my enquiry, stillness responds to my touch.

Now, so stillness speaks you could say, or burns, lights up.

We are One, multi-dimensional, alive, energetic being.

We could use words like God, Creator, Source and any of the other basic names associated with that.

As I Am eating a really, really delicious meal, I Am reminded to chew slowly and savor every bite, thereby making my relationship with energy more intimate, more deep.

Intimate here, I could also use from your lover, we draw inspiration from each other.

We give courage to forage for unfelt choices and slowly savor every bite.

Every time we come to a new understanding of a relationship within the whole, we operate in a new dimension.

Practice consciously being with Source, with energy.

Life encourages this.

Energy is the source of all existence- pure potential is the void and stillness of energy.

Nothing speaks, or stillness, pure potentiality, void, everything and nothing is Source, energy, God.

What makes me happy is to reiterate what I have heard that makes me happy and gives my Life, my energy.

And gives me Life, gives me energy.

What I learn or remember, are those reiterations, and what harms me in relationships to the point that everything is related.

What I love most so far is my conversation with Life, with friends, with energy.

Everything is an energetic aspect.

What we hear smell, taste, touch, all interactions.

The whole interacts.

We are One big family which includes our void, our energetic aspects.

Life itself continually reiterates this message.

13

THIRTEEN

How wonderful it is to meet again and have this opportunity to sit together.

Interacting, within this river of ours, our river easily carries all debris, all our thoughts and feelings.

Our flow spins, our world is a perfectly balanced one...

One who's tendency is Life.

When we speak of beauty and horror, we keep true to this perfect balance.

I see myself inclined to see beauty, to see the silver lining, my silver lining, even knowing on occasion of horror (as some call it).

It benefits me to see beauty, to see Life's polarities as Life living.

And it is ever our goal, wellness.

We live and we prefer beauty.

Can I experience horror as beauty?

And since we are living a balanced Life, both polarities get equal attention always.

And we do what we must, we play our part, one of us is an optimist, one of us is a pessimist.

Some experience drama and pain, some experience happiness and relief.

I must admit that I experience both and all.

All here meaning me here, seems to indicate there are additional dimensions to living a Life of polarity.

Because I just said I experience both and all.

So, there is definitely an additional dimension.

A Life where we acknowledge polarity and live from a broader bigger point of view.

My imaginary friends, our imaginary numbers is central to our wholeness.

Whole, h-o-l-e within our wholeness.

Our wholeness has a big hole in the middle.

This is funny.

Interesting Life when we are nothing, we want to be something.

And when we are something, we want to be nothing.

Very mysterious and for now our Life cycles.

So, death is the road to awe and from nothing springs Life.

I paint my picture, sing my song, dance my dance.

So when I Am prompted for a response, there is one.

And is ever beautiful, all Life is beauty in every way we experience it.

We call our Life with every word, thought, and feeling.

We live it thus and beautiful is our flow as we grow and add our multidimensional, blended lives.

Incorporating our lessons, our experiences into this eternal tapestry including now more potently my imagination.

What do I see now?
What does my character contribute to our landscape?
It is a shade of green, a splat of red, a fiery orange yellow all expressions of our/my wholeness, our Oneness, where our home is, my family and friends are.
Ever here with just a call.

Thank you, Life, most mysterious beauty.
I feel your love, your embrace, your support, my nourishing touch.
Hunger, my built-in suffering and you come along and feed me.
Did I ask?

Yes, my suffering asked.
Did you notice?
Yes, even in your darkest hour.
We are always with you...
And when am I alone?

Who am I?
What am I?
Who are we?

When we are talking, touching, communicating... we are conscious, consciously acting.
Express myself, express yourself, interacting with energy, acknowledge and express.
Ways of expressing seeming separateness, aloneness maybe seeming.
You can forget and I Am always here.
I can appear as form, thought, feelings and we are always together.
My hunger calls you and you come.

When I express affection for you, you become more loveable by all, especially by yourself.
Have confidence in your Life.
Have confidence in your Life experience so far, it will serve you well.
We are everything you know now.

So let us reiterate who we are.
Let us add what we want to make more obvious who we are.
Remember and I can help.
You can help me by reminding me.
What?

Become more obvious, remember, practice.
Remember space.
Let us add what we want to make more obvious, who we are.
To make more obvious who I Am, what we are.
... Very big one is space.

Items previously unnoticed just around the corner, energy, Oneness, closeness embraced by embraced by nothing.
A feeling of submergence, being touched.
We all experience Oneness all the time.
Consciously participating is our opportunity.
I notice that everything plays its part willingly and choicelessly.

So, I ask, what is my part?
I notice that I may choose, that I have some choices.
I see that some have chosen.
Life says that I may choose, have choices.

Thank you for sitting with me so patiently so continuously, it is called devotion.
Attention is a sign of affection.

When it comes from Life, we call it love.
Life's space around me is my embrace, intertwines me everywhere...
every limb and surface area, every thought and feeling, every cell,
atom, and electron.

My what?
What will fill in with detail who I Am, what we are.
What will I choose what will I imagine, my what is.
How will I imagine and fill in with detail?
... Interplay with energy?

What food nourishes me, heals me?
What song will I sing?
What dance will I dance?

My what?
My heart song.
My why?
Devotion to Life, my Life, your Life, our Life, our One Life.

This is my Oneness practice including now my separate pieces, seemingly separate yet never so, ever One produced from stillness, nothing,
subtle energy, all power, all intelligent, wise, playful, mischievous... so
I have heard.

I live.
I live very attentive now.
I Am all this, my experience is this.

My river runs deep.
Wow!

Yin and yang opposites are constantly embraced by nothing.
Wuji is a word for this interactive Life.
We are songs in the symphony of Life.
Anything that comes from memory comes from Life in response to an inquiry.
Wuji, energy work.
Instructions to padawans, to students. to learners... any way you do it is correct.
Moving toward beauty is encouraged.

Perfection via the elements of the execution of our movements, our forms, our interactions, our play.
Basically, it seems to be helpful to reiterate what you already know, what we already know.
This is in reference to inspiration, inspiration from Life itself and how we provide our function, play our role, our service.

I have chronic feelings of appreciation, love, eagerness, and joy.

14

FOURTEEN

Aahhh ever and always together- on a phone call, between our distances, this distance, these distances... seeming.
Where we can hear each other and even feel each other.
Our relationship with Life with energy will give us a sense of direction and values to live by.
And our food choices will give us a good body to enjoy Life with.

From good to better, to best ever, and from faith to belief, to experience to our eternal relationship, our Divine chemistry, body, energy, Life, Spirit.

Help is available ...ever.
Like photosynthesis, minerals, water, friends, medicinal herbs, and mushrooms, how intimate with Life will we allow ourselves to be?
... Our eternal friendship.

Be easy and kind with ourselves and with others, one step at a time.
Share your point of view.
Be your uniqueness.
Our intimate Life, our eternal friendship.
Have a good time with your pain and suffering if you must- paint,

scream and record it so we all may see and hear.
See your painting and hear your scream.
I want to hear your song.
Let us dance.
Let us play.

Let us dance and play, being ever mindful of our friendship when alone and together.
Interesting we are even capable of saying, "alone."
And how many small steps did it take?
And who responded to our asking?
How soon or quickly did I notice your response?

When did I notice, in a very personal and intimate way, Life reaching out to me?
And one day I recognized your response and remembered my friend... again.
Having had many close conversations before with strangers, friendly strangers.
Strangers with different faces, and names, under many different circumstances, and step-by-step, experience-by-experience.

I see our lineage now, our common ground, our family, and friends.
Friendly strangers, ha, and I wondered why.
Life, Source, God, energy, void, pure potential, soul, all are connections, all are relationships, all souls touching.
Our tree of souls, tree of Life, from leaves to branches, to trunk and roots, to sky to earth.
I have chronic feelings of appreciation, love, eagerness, and joy.

The Source of the Life I live comes from an underlying essence, deeper than my body and mind, my inspiration.
I Am inspired by my Source.

I Am inspiration for my Source by the choices I make from my point of view, our point of view…

Reactivate…

Clarity…

With…

Relaxed states…

Alkaline states- foods that promote those states.

Feeling and thinking better attracts feeling and thinking better and new opportunities.
Restore enzyme balance, digestion… probiotics, daily.
Friends are, we are, food for each other.
We nourish each other, food friends… ha-ha!

What is our experience?
I Am part of my whole seemingly separate always One whole.
My thoughts influence my Life.
We are worthy.

My feelings are my experience, my thoughts influence my feelings, my feelings also include my senses, my five senses, my physical senses.

My testimony is that everything is Life's Source, everything, every experience.
The space between us is everything also.
You, my friends, inspire me by showing me newly noticed aspects of myself.
Inclusively our words, endow or produce feelings that may be more

likeable or more nourishing than a separate point of view.

So, it is the house or my house.
My family my friends.
My part to play my song, our dance, our purpose.
Every part's part is for the whole, so my part is and our part, as we share what we notice, nourishes us, is helpful, kind, considerate.
It is being, playing our part, and it is best when in an inclusive nature from a holistic Oneness perspective.

I Am an aspect of yourself who loves you and I will never be the same, meaning we flow and are ever new and the same.
This is why, this is how, it is why, it is how because we are always everything.

And so, even though presented anew, when you show me your point of view, it is familiar it is true, and that feeling, the familiarity can always be new, as we flow ever on.
How did we discover that we are in love?
We paid so much attention to the Divine, to our Life Source, that one day we noticed the Divine or Source was paying constant attention to me.
To you, to us.
We are our gift to each other, we nourish you.

First, we discover we are separate, and we live our lives here.
Then we discover we are whole, and we live our lives here...
step by step by step...

15

FIFTEEN

Is hope physical?
... Any imagined state or living with a certain imagined state?
Yes.

For us for now we live our imagination, our hope shows.
And when we look out, when we look, when we notice, we see with
our imagination.
Can I see hope?
Interesting response, "have I forgotten?"
What have I just been reminded of with asking "can I see hope?"
Hope disappears when I remember who I Am.

When I Am reminded by my friends and remember who we are.
Yes, hope may replace despair on our sleepy bed.
Now awake, playing with my friends, laughter has replaced hope.

Who are our friends?
Our body, our food, energy consciousnesses, all very alive and interactive as we nourish each other with our attention.

How will we choose to interact as we play together?

As we live ever on?
And as for this vast space between us all, that embraces us and responds to our needs.

How will we choose to interact?
Alive as we all are, our space and our places.
All vital and eternal allowing our interactions.

Tempo, beat, harmony, do you see me now?
With your mind, with your imagination, recreating us anew.
Will we call each other by our names?
How intimate are we with each other?
Will we acknowledge our make-believe as our Life?
And as our friendship flowing?
Playing ever on?

Hi energy.
Hi Life.
Hi food.
Hi cucumber.
Hi silica.
Hi hope.
Hi goji.

Hi DNA, may I turn you on?
My energy, my feeling frequency touches you, my lovely antennae.
And you awake.
Now we see more.
Our capabilities soar.
DNA activation as we up our vibration with our intimate imagination.
Long time friends reappear.

Hi love.
Hi curiosity.
Hi strength.
Hi vigor.
Hi food.
Hi Life.

Let us play!
What is new?
An opportunity to see you anew.
Knowing, noticing, and acknowledging.
Humble bow, playful now.
Who am I?
Who are we?
We are Life, still and flowing, at rest and awake.
My chest rises and falls with burning pressure inside.
Relaxed creativity, imaginary, flowing, flowing imagination...
peaceful, very dark... nothing... words... only words?

Ah and sounds, vibrations, frequencies, we frequent each other (ha).
From our intimate, deep, dark depths.
Our harmonies rise, and Life appears.
What are we really?

Let us feel for a while, let our sounds roll on a while.
While we sit and feel.
Feel what we have imagined... and let longing rest.
Place our attention on what rests next to your appearance.

What rests next to your appearance?
This space by your chakra, between our chakras?
...this mighty embrace so dark, allowing appearances...
So dark, now we notice our light, alive space nourishing, bringing forth Life, energy, sound, bubbling brook, fountain of Life, unseen for now.

Imagined, curious, friendly, revealing and hiding.
I lay deeply emerged, your kiss on my body.
Our interaction, your touch, my Life, our experience-
Ravished ever, well-loved.
Alive, unknowable, unknowable new-nesses all at once.
Ever new, young and old, all at once.
The hero of our own adventure... the heroine of our own adventure.

I know we each see the Divine from our own point of view and from here we make our choices.
What I say is simply repeating what you already know, it is just very nice to hear it again.
It is very nice to hear the same thing from different sources.
This establishes the eternal nature of Life.
To reiterate ...abundantly.
Life is so redundant it is eternal.

How visceral, tangible, experiential... how real every day, every moment is my relationship with the Divine, with Source!
And what is our evidence?
We establish our communication, we sit together, we notice, we acknowledge, we bow, we interact, we play, sing our harmonies and dance. We notice our communication; we acknowledge our communication, and our hearts live on, and our heartsong becomes self-evident. We interact.
We are interacting... ask, inquire, interview.

My Divine is obliged to respond, my normal has improved, my emptiness is now consciously included in my new normal Life.
My stillness is now consciously included in my new normal.
My silence, my absolute is now consciously included in my new normal Life.
How obvious can I make my obvious?
Ha.

What shall I do?
Consciously and choicelessly decide my Life is inherent, innate.
So now I consciously include nothing and everything when I move.
...when I move my thought...when I move my emotion...my body.

I recognize holistically who I Am.
And yes, everything is conscious, because we reciprocate attention.
I Am made of nothing, pure potentiality.
I appear, my appearance is noticed, and I know a bit more about my intimate, eternal variety and innate motion- as in inhalation and expansion...
as in exhalation and contraction.

There is enough evidence when we ask and Life responds, what are we?
Yes, we have forgetting, and we have remembering even though we cannot see our space, our space can be seen.
Interesting space.
Sublime space how beautifully, deeply traumatic, dramatic I can be when unrevealed.
I do not know.
I do not have to know.
I can let it go and see me.

Our appearance world is perfectly balanced when said like this, has a

different effect an intellectual effect, let us say.
My experiential feeling aspect is living wild.

Let Life live, experiencing wholeness.
I thought we were done for now?
We are never done.
We move without consent.
Lovely to repeat and yet we are no longer there.
Lovely to repeat, because I forgot.
Lovely to repeat, because now I remember.
Lovely to repeat, I remember, I forgot.
I see me, I feel me, I notice me.

My heartsong, my song and dance, how sublime, how Divine.
I wonder what Divine means?
I Am curious, I respond.
Follow what appears behind the curtain.

16

SIXTEEN

And I would like to respond, please take it lightly.

Life is paying so much attention to the Divine until you notice, the Divine is constantly paying attention to you.

Always has, is now, and always will.

Now I, blended Life, use the word Life and the word Divine, to point at our extra ordinary Life.

Extra ordinary when I notice and include, with my five senses, our energetic aspects and also how our five senses and our energetic aspects play.

What sounds are made?

And here I Am not talking about a sound I hear with my ears, but Life itself as a symphony... every sense, all playing at once, experienced as our Life and using the word Divine for me, blends these things a little better.

Like a good-tasting meal or a wonderfully presented symphony.

Anyway, we have our storms and our sunny days- both in weather, and in thoughts, and feelings, and in exchanges with each other.

Again, a very more than, appears Life, and when I look at this space right next to your ear, Life loves and appreciates this noticing, and reciprocates and says, "ah, you noticed!"

We have this energetic exchange, the inspired, actual exchange, the inspiration - here is energy... is very energetic in that, ah, my eyes light up.
I see more clearly.
I hear more clearly, food tastes better...
your kiss ...thrills me more, your fragrance ...
thrills me more.

So, components, additional components then, since our thoughts and feelings are so very interactive with our senses, and our lives, and our friends, interactive with our friends.
This is a very creative Life in the sense that I have my imagination which ...
I should say we have imagination.
I definitely agree we have imagination and from a let us say, meal prep point of view.
It is very easy to see we do, because we have to come up with something to eat for a meal if we have friends... and family, children, or even just to enjoy something- there is a certain amount of imagination.

Wellness, generally we are well, in a sense that Life lives.
We may look at the bits and pieces and say well, "that Life, there is a dead bug, well" we are not looking at a piece, we are looking at a holistic experience.

Yes, I have dead skin cells sluffing off my arm right now.
Yet, I also enjoy how softly the wind caresses my flesh, my skin.
When I imagine the spaces between us which produces our harmonies- my intention more, my practice, would be, aligning with my wellness.

Me, you, we, us, them, I, all expressions of our Oneness; different flavors, colors, sounds, aromas, tastes of my Oneness.
How will we greet what touches us?
From whose touch?
What does it feel like to wind to touch my skin?
What does wind know of touching me?
And what do I know of being touched by the wind?
Well, when this happens the feeling is mutual.

And we start our conversation... ah, thank you.
Our senses is a good place to initiate alignment with our wellness.
It is so immediate, under our noses, so to speak.
From here we can carry our alignment to our thoughts.

Our thoughts here are- say that because it is easy to align with the wellness of our physical nature, especially when I look at... well I mean... okay... we want, let us say we have a thought we want to align with- and yes, and yet we ignore it... well, the practice would be to include all, because all is Life and all and it is all us, all me.
And we can make it personal every time.

So, alignment here with wellness means, looking at something that is easy to align with, so let us say let us look at something green.
Well, all of a sudden bingo!
I like it, it feels good.
Or any color, let us say.
You may have favorite colors so let us use our favorite things to remember our best feelings, and then take that momentum to every thought, as they arise, as a practice.

Align your thoughts with the choiceless choice that is your Life, integrate it, blend it.
Food and eating is an expression of this.

Our dialogues are our nourishment.
Tending to our relationship is our primary purpose.
Let us be about noticing each other, our friends.
This is how it works.
Remember, practice, be with your friend, go and plan with your friends.

This unveiled Life, the beloved unveiled, the Beloved as Source, Life, unmanifest, formless.
Add this noticing to your experience as you go about your day.
I Am the beloved and the Belov-ed.
As we practice and remember our energy shows this, we show this to each other.
This is how it works.
And this is how it is in the moment for now, how I see it.
We can help, I know it.

It is like being in love, we know it- from this point I can meet the world, from this tiniest point.
What is the treasure there behind this which, behind this thought that I may suddenly, momentarily tend to ignore, or resist, or oppose?
I always have my resources at hand to play with and be curious about anything that comes.
Previously I answered, "Who am I?"
Now I know who I Am and my purpose for me here.
Express yourself.
Life is a big pun.
Let us see what is on the other side of the hill of dogma.
Let us see what is on the other side of the abyss of a flat world.

Will someone in authority please say, "everything is alright!"
All is well.
You are loved.
You are alive.
Life is acting here.
This is helpful to say these things to reiterate and to confirm Life.
To confirm Life with our song, with our heartsong.

Ask yourself, what makes me so responsive to you?
What makes me notice how responsive you are to me?
There is more to you than meets the eye or is it only what I can see for now?
What will the next moment reveal?
I would love a conversation with you- a slow long one, that will allow for pauses and many questions as they arise, and to encourage deeper acknowledgements of who I Am, who we are.
Namaste.

Thank you for being so magnanimous with your attention, with your responses, with yourself, with your noticing.
It is all alright.
We are all alright.
(Love that) mischievous and innocent way of saying, it is all alright.
... The so called bad, or resisted, or disallowed.
Our exchange is supposed to be mysterious.
To softly touch the mystery until it is noticed, understood, revealed...

Observe, interact, imagine... my interaction is observing my feelings as I observe my preferences.

We are meditating here a little bit, about our connectedness...

Our noticing of each other, and honoring, and acknowledging, taking our noticing deeper, interacting, playing together, sharing our thoughts and imaginings... as we notice our aliveness and carry that noticing to everything we notice as being alive and conscious.
Everything knows how to interact with us, with each other.
Our flow, so alive, so intimate, so dynamic...
We could say our voices are Oms... aum... every expression...
so easy and intricate, easy in that it allows our touch, our interaction...

The sun may be far away and yet, on uncovered skin we are actually touching the sun...
In touching does not seem to have any distance, necessarily involved.
Physically, let us say the sun is actually touching me because my skin, my flesh responds.
As to the wind, and an aroma, where did that aroma drift in from?
From a flower across the pond or the garden?
We do touch each other all the time and distance reveals connected-ness, connection, relationship.

How can distance (this is so funny, when I look at it alone) oh, you are so far away, and where are we looking for love?
In the memory?
In the touch?
In the feeling?
In the relationship?
These are our feelings, our touching, our relationships, our memories, and we can always make it personal and say "my."

17

❧

SEVENTEEN

We consciously participate with the puppeteer, asking who Am I, sets us into our current from possibly, an eddy.
We all inspire each other to look at our Life from my own point of view.
We all inspire each other to look at our Life from my point of view.
I Am inspired when I Am enjoying your heartsong, many heartsongs.

I enjoy my favorite ones so much each time I play them.
Now I Am enjoying my heart's song, my heartsong, finally.
Now I enjoy my heartsong each time I play it.
Life inspires itself... first you inspire me then I inspire you.

We are all, we are well when we can answer "Yes!!"
Now what happens when I eat something?
Is my GMO popcorn transmutable?
Or... abstain from eating it?

A question for a breatharian, what of my five senses role as you are nourished?
What is really happening when my sense of aroma is engaged?
How do we smell something?

What is this functions role?
What of all my senses when I enjoy food?
And yet as a breatharian would abstain from eating it I imagine the aroma of it nourishes.
And the seeing of it nourishes.
Maybe the touching of it... I do not know.

What is the definition or how do we, how does this function of smelling work?
So, I inhale, and exhale and I Am very mindful and consciously participate.
For now, I enjoy the taste and the chewing and the digestion.
Some say the energy alone of breathing nourishes them.
I wonder what fragrances are included in this nourishment.
What memories and the energies of our memories-
I wonder how they participate?
Thanks for the memory... integrate the energy...

This whole Life is here to birth only you...this whole Life is here to birth only me...as deeply as possible.
I feel into this as we all say and meditate on our reality.

What is a true experience?
This is a true experience.
Today I reiterate, I Am going to stay the course with Source.
With my Source, with your Source, with our Source.
I ask, and I acknowledge.
I ask to work together.
I acknowledge we are working together- me, my Source, and I...ha-ha.
We cocreate, we play you and I.
I ask you.
I acknowledge you are our manager.

I acknowledge Source is my manager.
How beautiful we are.

I.
I is a Oneness symbol.
I Am.
I Am ... our Oneness... our not knowing... our letting Life live... our wildness, our input from the wild side, not knowing... yet living.
Our purpose allows influence by others... so remember, practice, allowing teaches.

What would satisfy forever?
Why do we want to be helpful?
Why do we want to be confident?
To feel confident?
Confidence, satisfaction...this is why I want to be helpful, to feel satisfied.

Why do I want to be happy?
To feel good.
Why do I want to express my highest purpose?
To be effective.
Why do I want to be effective?
To be healthy.
Why do I want to be healthy?
To feel good.
So, we just came around.

Again, why do I want to feel good?

To live my inspired Life.

Here we notice our holistic nature.

What makes me happy then?

Feeling confident, feeling satisfied.

This is living our connected state.

Confidence, a result of noticing and acknowledging our connected state... ever connected.

This is very satisfying.

This is very satisfying for now.

For now, is ever now...and Life is a dangling carrot as we are enticed to flow ever on.

Rest is very satisfying.

Eating satisfies my hunger.

Eating the best ever satisfies my health- my joy, my greatest highest purpose, my effectiveness, our beauty.

Feeling good satisfies all.

Feeling good satisfies all lacks, all hungers, all bodily requirements.

My body is more than I see or understand today.

My thinking my thoughts...how do I feel?

I observe... did that thought support my confidence?

Do I feel good?

Observe and practice.

Breathe.

How did that thought make me feel?

What do I choose to think now?

As we enjoy our connected inspired state, I encourage us to have pen and paper at our side in our hands in every moment so that our walking meditation may... Inspire us upon reading it.

So, let us be able to write at a moment's notice and not have to know anything... and be inspired, and breathe, and practice, and reiterate, and share.

I Am looking for an experience that you may not have experienced before.
Ever notice how we are nothing and then something?
Ever notice how we are nothing and then something?
My part in this task is to notice I Am breathing, notice my heart beating.
This is my heartsong.
Every instant you are a stranger.
I know nothing about you even after we meet and talk, and we call each other friends I could see you as a stranger.
It is easy to love a stranger because you do not know him/her.
Moment by moment I see you anew as the Divine One, as the unknown, unknowable, beautiful stranger.

We are all at certain stages of our blossoming, a symphony of appearances.
Let us play pretend
Who are you?
I Am a friend.
You are not my friend I do not know you.
Then I Am a stranger.
It is easy to love you because I do not know you.
Who is the stranger?
Let us not know.
I Am that which you do not know, yet here Am I right before you.
Now I Am your friend because now you know me as yourself.

And this applies to all our relationships.
Our air, thank you.
Our water, thank you.

Our food, thank you.
I Am Life, is an advocate for well-being.

Energy responds to our thoughts- our emotions tell us what my thoughts are creating and indicate my reality.
Ninety-nine per cent of my relationships, people I talk with, are friends.
One per cent are strangers.
None are enemies.

"I Am myself a permanent principle.
I have heard of my real characteristics.
I now visualize myself beyond a shadow of a doubt.
This is my enlightenment.
I make myself visualize my real nature of permanent peace.
And now I realize that I have always been this peace."
~ Sri Atmananda

Now my joy is visualizing my real nature.
I visualize myself as I really Am.
Notice, acknowledge, interact.
Confirm, clarify compassionately, feel about others, remember all One Life.
We all know really, everyone and everything is in essence speaking about our One Life.
We are all living our One Life.
We are all in this together.
We all play our part willingly and choicelessly.
So, personally I set my attention that I may acknowledge your words and actions as a reiteration of what is our One Life.
Personally I set my attention that I may acknowledge your words and actions as a reiteration of what is our One Life.

This is because each one of us has as our primary focus- what do I feel right now?

What Am I feeling?

My objective, my noticing, helps me to understand where I Am relative to where I want to be, with respect to what Am I feeling now... and what do I want to feel really?

So, I employ my memory of my favorite things and approach my best feelings ever.

One Life, we are living our One Life.

Aspects of our One Life have a unique view, and that view is always One Life's view cherished and honored for its unique role and purpose.

My unique role and purpose is always blended as my One Life.

My purpose and role is obvious while my One Life from my uniqueness is mysterious.

My unique role and purpose is always blended as my One Life.

Blessings.

Blessings.

Shall I believe you have faults?

Ha...we are all there is, and it is our One Life.

18

EIGHTEEN

Every aspect is the whole and as a flow, so then is our conversation. Every aspect is the whole and is a flow, so then is our conversation for everything is conscious.

Okay let us look.

Because we see each other when we look, and we recognize each other as a person, and pretty much know when we speak we will hear each other and carry on a conversation by speaking with words we both understand.

Now, we hear our conversation only in silence, every word we exchange is automatically spoken in our native tongue and in the background a melody is playing.

The melody is silent, it is our flowing stream.

Back to our conversation...

Artistically let us say, over there where the sun is dancing on the water, and only over there because this is what we observe, and the wind must also be splashing about over there, so many sparkles, beautiful to my eyes.

They are having a conversation, and we just listened in.

Okay, got distracted.

So, our conversation, face to face, continues even between our sentences, those silent moments.

Let us look at our silent conversation more closely.

What do we have in mind?

And paying attention at first, for a little while until we see an opportunity to join in... an opportunity to join in to the conversation.

What am I talking about?

Let us recognize that our silent conversation is an actual conversation and treat it as such, kindly.

A conversation between friends!

Let us have some fun with this and play a while here.

And we can talk out loud too.

Let us include in our conversation with friends, silence as a friend, and what would we bring to such a conversation?

Silence here as I mentioned is the space between sentences.

The space between words.

The space in a musical composition that embraces every note.

So, what would we bring to such a conversation?

... Our most intimate curiosities.

For in this silence, in this space, this unknown knowingness, this peace, this quiet, this stillness, it is really easy to bring our intimate curiosities.

Because no one hears these out loud, although everyone knows what they are in silence, our most intimate curiosity-

Those curiosities.

Long contemplated, brought forward step by step until we approach our precipice of pure potential.

Our unknown answer, our next question to be formulated.

Now silence confidently steps in and supplies us with a morsel so delightful that we are nourished once again, and flow ever on together.

Our friendship renewed and with nary a concern with what energy propels us on, gives us our Life.

We know we are together, enjoying each other's company, our play and the wonder of our next adventure before us.

When the world was flat did it really matter?
There is always more going on than meets the eye.

Pick someone, anybody, and have a conversation with them.
They can be anywhere in the world and see what happens.
I generally choose someone I currently interact with, what they have written, sung, posted, or something I remember from my past, imme-diate past, and older.
In the past and even now we are focused mostly on the good and the bad, the polarity of appearances.

Our opportunity here is looking at the balanced perspective of good/bad and our seesaws' appearance shifts to our flow.

Perspective from balance shows an enhanced view of our Life, Life to-gether, our world.
This is our individual discovery.
All Life is singing this song silently in our ears, ever... listen, be curious and ask.
Notice Life's response and appreciate your relationship, your friend-ship, our friendship.
Now we can play and be in wonder of our great love.

So, pay attention to how I feel now.
How do I feel now?
Warmly embraced.
The spaces, the silence, the stillness between my thoughts, my feelings, between my molecules, between my atoms, electrons, protons, between my thoughts and feelings.

Ask yourself frequently, what am I feeling now?
Honor this, honor the responses.
Honor that which shows up.
Notice, acknowledge, interact.
I honor my feelings.
I honor my Life.
I honor what I Am feeling now, by noticing, acknowledging, interacting.
Breathe!

I shall do what I must for you are in my world.
Our lyrics, our songs, our heartsongs could be played, sung as they are, or you could embellish with your unique Life experience.
Embellish, blend... I believe that would be better.

Unacknowledged love helps me to allow my noticing is not a choice, my curiosity is not a choice, my yearning is innate, is part of my functioning.
You must respond because I ask it of you.
Because I have asked.
Look at your connection, look at our connectedness, practice our connectedness.
Disconnected- separate- protectiveness... protective?
Your whole system function- ever connected.

Tend to your emotional journey.

Follow that, decide what you feel best at.
Be that.
Sing your heartsong.
Inspire with your heartsong.
Catalyze with your heartsong.
These words are for you, for us.
I enjoy them also, but they are for you for your noticing of your gifts
and using your gifts, your best gifts.
For your gifts... are One Life.

We all serve our purpose- our purpose supports Life.
Inspire yourself.
I imagine that these words do that.
They inspire you.
They inspire me.
Use them or use your own words or blend them, these words are for
you.
Life is everything, my favorite things, we are One... breathe.
I see your beauty.
I see your eyes.
I see you.

I Am noticing we bless and are blessed.
By noticing we bless our thoughts our feelings.
They arise from our space, our quiet place.
Our noticing are signs of affection.
The void, pure potentiality, ineffable reality moves, speaks, expresses.
Of its imagining we appear, I appear.
What is the foundation from which you make your inquiry?
Can you recall any experience of love?
That remembering is your foundation experience.
Notice, are you now at peace?
At rest?

When you notice, remembering, recalling an experience of love?
Bless and honor your memory and your state.
Now you can ask your dark questions.

Thank you, thank you, thank you.
Our noticing of each other is our blessing, our connection.
This flow of energy... signs of affection, attention.
Thank you for noticing.
Thank you for acknowledging.

Humble bow.
We now know we are loved and well connected for we have been re-minded.
And when we forget, all Life responds and reminds us... ever.

19

NINETEEN

Interesting how we get clearer on the working of our lives and on our purpose.

Now that I see that other things have purpose, it is easier for me to allow thoughts that give me purpose- thoughts that point to my purpose.

I will think those thoughts now and see what bubbles to the top as my purpose.

I Am asking for a very, very, slightly closer relationship- relationships with everything-

With Life and everything in it, especially the ineffable expressions.

Life's ineffable expression of Life experiencing itself as me, you, everything, as it appears and disappears, and more even than that.

Our one expression, and well said as my One expression, as we all say at the same time, "My One expression."

So, we are, or I Am, as we can say both, since we are One, ah-ha.

I Am an aspect of my, I have my unique expression as Life has envisioned Itself as me and my environment.

As Life looks through my eyes and through all of Its appearances instantaneously.

Life's symphony plays its next note.

As we interact, Life experiences Itself anew... Life lives.

Life is alive!

Life is energy, vibration, resonances, frequencies and harmonies.

Our five senses and more are Life's experience of its own symphony or work.

Life's opus is void and galaxies and all therein, you, me, animals, plants, minerals, air, water, all everything and nothing and more is Life.

We express ourselves and gain experience of ourselves and on and on it goes.

By our interactions we confirm, clarify compassionately what and who we are.

Where am I, is an interesting question.

Can I recall any experience of love?

No?

Adrift in our One Life with no memory of any experience of love?

And yet, right now, I begin to <u>feel</u> my experience- my whole body and being immersed in my One Consciousness.

I begin to feel buoyancy, support.

I breathe, and air fills my lungs.

I relax.

I feel again and notice a subtle embrace within.

I open my eyes and what appeared dim is now brighter.

Life seems clearer.

I feel warmer... my buoyancy feels subtly assuring.

I relax.

I take another breath... I feel Life coming into my body and My Being awakens!

Can I, this moment, recall any experience of love?

Yes!

Why am I saying all this?
Because I want to be happy.
I want to feel good.
I want to be well.
How is it possible?
It is our nature.

Innately I live.
Thrival is built in.
Happiness is Life's intention.
Happiness is my intention now, always, and this is why we feedback via our senses and our thoughts, and are able to recognize, yes- that thought did feel better.
My aim... miss the mark... produces contrast.

It is not my job to sing like Celine Dion, but I do have my heartsong, and I enjoy experiencing her sing.
We have different interests and develop certain capabilities, and others can enjoy them.
I do not have to provide every need or supply every purpose.
All I want to do is be my purpose as fully as possible.
We want to experience each other.

I like to notice as I wake up with a gentle hand, this is how a warrior is set out into the world. there is so much respect between cooperative components.
Our embrace, my vibrational field, I show resonance, my note is playing, this is how my task is done.

Now I do my task.
I make the most of my current moment, interaction, the fire is out,
my healing begins.

I have to say some words so my face can appear.
I feel the aura of our embrace, of our interaction.
Now remember that I play as an interactive component within my
vibrational field, and I remain untouched, for I Am here everywhere
and mostly nowhere now.
So how do we talk about our experience?
Yes, I Am looking for experiential input, interaction, playing.
It is helpful and enjoyable for me to interact with you.

Again, what is my experience?
I feel embraced.
I notice more and more that everything reiterates and reciprocates.
My stillness responds to enquiry, Life responds.
I confess my relationship with that which responds.
I can say I love you, however my experience is our attention on each
other. Devotion, interaction for now a private matter, for basically my
interaction, our interactions, are noticing responses to my inquiries-
very nourishing.
I notice our blossoming, when is a blossoming flower more beautiful?
Now?
How about now?
Maybe even now, as we grow and blossom into our fullness, an eternal
flow.

It sounds like we all know what we are talking about here, what we,
our unique experiences, our sharing of unique experiences.
And we are all sharing about the same thing in our own unique way-
since there is only one thing to talk about- there is only one of us talking, and expressing, and sharing.

Acknowledge and honor what we notice as our own reality and our own Divine Reality, to put it in an ineffable multidimensional reality.

Divine is nothing special, just extremely ordinary, everything and nothing in contrasting relationships... that appear infinitely beautiful, and blossom eternally- blossoming, and then blossoming, and then blossoming.
And from our noticing we participate creatively and yes, we are beautiful.

To make it personal and experiential we can say, yes, I Am, "I Am That."
... maybe, someone said that.
Let us have some fun, let us play pretend.
We are together, apart.

Be friendly, share our experience, trust in providence, your friend, and friends which have, is, are always with us.
It is all in my mind.
Trust in your friends, they are always with you.
They are your family, your tribe, your pod.
Let go, allow, trust.

Everyone and everything is the Divine so everyone and every appearance qualifies, everyone and every appearance qualifies as a reminder of who I Am.
So, every regular same, ordinary, familiar- you, me, dog, cat, cow, house, car, telephone, organic, inorganic, stream, true, garden; what shift is that?

Life eternally reiterates who, what we are, what will be, what is my re-iteration?

What creative aspect is my play- what do I want really?
What has my Life set me up for?
My ineffable expression, words that dance around my ineffable expression.

Practice, repeat, read, imbibe, be nourished.
Journal.
Read your journal.
Read your words and practice repeating them.

We are One Source.
And when we awake from physical sleep into conscious sleep, we die into awe and Life springs forth.
One can say anything, and it is an expression of One Source, One Life.
Source says it awesomely... it is always right.
So, what is wrong?

Yes, this world is very physical and very malleable.
What relationship are we encouraged to seek first?
How willingly do I take your offered hand?
We are all innocent.
Our offering nourishes Life, My One Life.
Express fully.
Feel its flow.
Life must feed my hunger.
I Am eternally satisfying.

My One Life, express fully, express yourself, feel my flow.
Life must feed my hunger.
I Am eternally satisfying.
Ha-ha.
Our One Life, my One Life, express yourself fully, feel your flow... Life must feed your hunger.

I Am eternally satisfied- river flowing blessing peace, experience your-self.
Interaction is good, preferences arise, let us play.

Our Life is a motion.
It looks like a flow, a figure eight flow... a torus, appearing and disappearing, one event because there is one event, one moment now.
And in our one moment all appears.

Respond to every nudge, every noticing which is teaching you deep listening- this is deep listening.
We are practicing something we already know... we are practicing something we already know.
We are just bringing forth the fullness of our expressing, deepening our experience, our intimacy for the greater good, for the whole system, for the flow.

Meditate, imagine well, be with your friends, everything is our friend, be with and listen to each other and share and know who we are.

"Unable to perceive the shape of you, I find you all around me. Your presence fills my eyes with your love It *humbles my heart, for you are everywhere.*"

~ Hakim Sanai

RESOURCES

Influencers: Hafiz, Hakim Sanai, Nevil Goddard, Rumi, Sri Ramana Maharshi

Book: Benner, Joseph S. (1949, January 1). The Impersonal Life. DeVorss Publications:
Camarillo, CA

Channeling: Abraham Hicks: www.Abraham-Hicks.com
Channeling: Teachings of Ascended Masters: The Sumit Lighthouse - www.Tsl.org

Ancient Springs Retreat Center: www.ancientsprings.com

Lenore Culin: Attunement for Personal and Planetary Transformation, 23 minute video
www.Attunement.life

Danielle Hendryx: https://verdevalleymfr.com

Anne Lantry: www.anneshands.com
Anne Lantry: www.bodyalchemysedona.com

Pamela Wilson: Fellowship of the Heart: www.pamelasatsang.com

Rutury Temay: Ancient Springs Retreat Center:
www.ancientsprings.com
Rutury Temay: Tribal and non-Tribal Community, providing counseling services, educational programs and workshops:.
www.indioshuichol.org

Classical Music Influences: Chopin, Liszt, Mahler, Mozart, Strauss

Other Music Influences: Bluegrass, Blues, Cajun, Folk, Rock and Roll, Boogie Woogie

Movie: Entire Movie: "Lost Horizon" 1937 (made into film from the book by James Hilton, 1933). "Be Kind" is the main event.

"The Sound of Music:" The song, sung by Julie Andrews:

"I go to the hills when my heart is lonely.
I know I will hear what I've heard before.
My heart will be blessed with the sound of music.
And I'll sing once more."

Song: Ong Namo by Snatam Kaur

Your Journey Doesn't End Here...

Our Heartsong is the first of 144 upcoming books in the **Pass It On** series. Each story unlocks new insights and powerful lessons from life's most profound challenges. By sharing in the wisdom of others, you can find deeper understanding and renewed strength for your path. Check out these titles to be released in 2025 and don't miss our first box set of twelve, available during the 2025 holidays.

TRUCKIN' THROUGH TWO REALITIES - A schizophrenic truck driver's journey to retrieve our inherent wisdom. (A. Wessel)

WHISPERS FROM THE ANCIENT ONES - PART I - Reclaiming your power: The grace in forgiveness (E.C. Sanders)

THE RUNWAY RUNAWAY - Memoir of a Brazilian destitute street kid following God's breadcrumbs (W. Lima)

IN EVERY SOUL IS A SONG – PART I - Multi-dimensional healing and spiritual guidance from a near-death-experience to uplift every aspect of life (Rev. M. Lucas)

CAPRIS-CORN - The wisdom and karmic imprint of Capricorn in astrology (Rev. F. James)

DOWSING FOR BABIES - Simple dowsing and body-intuitive techniques to get answers to your questions (Q. Moore)

THE BOOT - An opera singer's rebellious journey:
From Mormonism to Namaste (Pen Name TBD)

www.ingramcontent.com/pod-product-compliance
Lightning Source LLC
Chambersburg PA
CBHW070756120626
46557CB00002B/618